DATE DUE			
MR3 0 95			

BR

DRAT THESE BRATS!

ALSO BY X. J. KENNEDY

The Beasts of Bethlehem

Brats

The Forgetful Wishing Well: Poems for Young People

Fresh Brats

Ghastlies, Goops & Pincushions

The Kite That Braved Old Orchard Beach:
   Year-Round Poems for Young People

(Margaret K. McElderry Books)

DRAT THESE BRATS!

X. J. KENNEDY

illustrations by James Watts

MARGARET K. McELDERRY BOOKS
NEW YORK

Maxwell Macmillan Canada
Toronto

Maxwell Macmillan International
New York Oxford Singapore Sydney

5567540

Margaret K. McElderry Books   Maxwell Macmillan Canada, Inc.
Macmillan Publishing Company   1200 Eglinton Avenue East
866 Third Avenue   Suite 200
New York, NY 10022   Don Mills, Ontario M3C 3N1

Macmillan Publishing Company is part of the Maxwell Communication
Group of Companies.
First edition   Printed in the United States of America
10 9 8 7 6 5 4 3 2 1   The text of this book is set in Baskerville.
The illustrations are rendered in pencil.
Library of Congress Cataloging-in-Publication Data
Kennedy, X. J.
   Drat these brats! / X. J. Kennedy ; illustrations by James Watts. — 1st ed.
      p.   cm.
   Summary: Forty-four humorous poems which describe the behavior of some
annoying children.
   ISBN 0-689-50589-2
   1. Children—Conduct of life—Juvenile poetry.   2. Children's poetry,
American.   [1. Behavior—Poetry.   2. American poetry.   3. Humorous
poetry.]   I. Watts, James, date, ill.   II. Title.
PS3521.E563D7   1993
811'.54—dc20   92-33686

Some of this matter first appeared in *Cayapooya Collage, Light, Sticks*, and
Robert Wallace's *Light Year* anthologies (Bits Press).

In the drugstore Hannah Hoover
Drank a vial of spot-remover
Which for people wasn't meant.

Anybody know where Hannah went?

Told to wash Pooch, awful Arch
Dipped the dog in laundry starch,
Making Pooch's hair stand stiffer—

Ain't that cute?
                    I beg to differ.

A time machine! Rob felt an itch
To jump inside and throw the switch.

That creaky crate cranked back through time
To when Earth was a ball of slime

And all creation but a blob—
Back when there wasn't any Rob.

To open cans of cola, Lil
Used her father's dental drill.

Of Dad's patients, none is willing
To endure another filling.

Sneaking in on soundless sneakers
    While her weary folks relax,
Wanda tiptoes to the speakers,
    Twists the volume up to max.

Windows shatter. Did a rock
    Flung by hand destroy the glass?
No way. Just a blast of Bach—
    Smashing, that B Minor Mass.

Snooping round the clinic, Craig
Stole a whole bubonic plague
That some scientist had bottled—

CRASH!

Craig, why so pale and mottled?

In the Rockies, reckless Basil
Frightens Father to a frazzle
Imitating big-horned sheep—
"Look, Dad! Watch this daring leap!"

From crag to crag he springs, but misses
And finds out all about abysses.

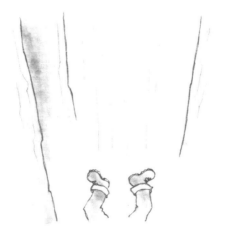

Maura poured some tranquilizer
   (Medicine for jumpy nerves)
   Into Mom's wild plum preserves—
Those who taste are none the wiser.
   They just sit and calmly smile
   An incredibly long while.

Basil in the jungle brake
Tripped upon a tropic snake,
Said, "Some fireman, I suppose,
Went away and left his hose.
Funny firehose—where's its nozzle?
I'll just take a look—"

Bye, Basil.

Home with seashore treasures, Trish
Slipped a juicy jellyfish
With an evil cackle down
Aunt Eve's backless evening gown—

Yuk! And yet that little smarty
Instantly pepped up the party.

Off the rooftop Cora Kotch
Tosses Father's costly watch.

"Dad, you're mad? What's wrong?" she cries.
"You're always saying, 'How time flies!'"

Campfire-cooking, Eloise
Fed a grizzly melted cheese
To find out did it like Welsh rarebit.

Eloise was what the bear bit.

Touring TV studios,
Left alone a moment, Rose
Yanked a plug and—consternation!
Sets blanked out across the nation.

Soap fans, having hung for weeks
In suspense, gave anguished shrieks,
But who was Cass's secret lover
They didn't (thanks to Rose) discover.

To make a good impression, Brent
Waded through the fresh cement
On the walkway to the garden,
Round his ankles felt it harden,
Stood there all day long until
Liberated by a drill.

Wallace fired his water pistol
At Mom's precious vase of crystal
Which fell, delicately tinkling,
All to pieces in a twinkling,
And, as well as he could do,
He reassembled it with glue.

"Oh well," sighed Mother. "I suppose
It's just right for a crooked rose."

Reed, who didn't reason well,
Hammered on a giant shell
That had washed in at low tide.
With a WHAM its lid sprang wide—

Good grief! Who'd have thought a scallop
Packed so powerful a wallop?

Emma, who enjoys a jape,
Lifts the latch and lets escape
A roaring bull, which catches Emma
On the horns of a dilemma.

For his nature project, Sherm
Raised a huge voracious worm
Which wove sticky silk all round him.

Weeks went by till we'd unwound him.

If you should tour a pyramid,
Do not do as Dudley did:

Do not pour your chocolate shake
Down a sacred rubied snake,

Do not hide Great-grandpa's truss
In some old sarcophagus.

Mind you walk a wiser path
Lest mean mummies rise in wrath.

At the duckpond Steff, that oaf,
Tossed the ducks an entire loaf.

Feathers flew. The water shook
From a duckish donnybrook,

While on shore, ducks kicked up dust,
Fighting over crumb and crust.

Steffan cackled in his glee:
"Who set off this battle? Me!"

But soon the brawlers, out of bread,
Started in on him instead,

Tweaking him with busy beaks—
Steff ate standing up for weeks.

Mountain-climbing in Peru,
Mel does what good kids don't do:

Flings stones at a bird of prey.
Pretty soon, to his dismay,

Mel is collared by a condor,
Flown afar, and left to wander.

Playing beaver, busy Keith
Tackled with his two front teeth
A redwood trunk. How hard he tried!—
Not knowing it was petrified.

Stewart with pea-shooter stirred
Up a snoozing bison herd
Which in little time indeed
Loudly started to stampede.

Some may like resentful bison,
But to Stew they proved pure p'ison.

You oughtn't to have made it, Bert,
Your monster gelatin dessert.

That slippery slab of sea-green slime
Has swallowed you.

                 (Yum! lemon-lime!)

Trish upon the railroad tracks
Poured a can of high-gloss wax.

Though the trains tried hard to brake,
Lots of stops they couldn't make.

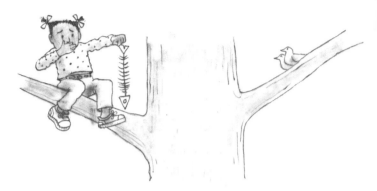

Lurking on the stream's bank, Claire
Pilfers salmon from a bear
Who soon finds out, resents her foul
Trick, and trees her with a growl
And makes her eat each stolen morsel
From lateral fin right down to dorsal.

With her felt pen Flo, that wretch,
Finishes a priceless sketch
Leonardo'd left undone.

Guards come swooping—

                              run, Flo, run!

At the wildlife sanctuary
Always-scoffing skeptic Gary
Jeers, "What fakes! You call *those* bogs?
Those alligators? Plastic logs!
Those hisses? Just a tape recording!"

Suddenly a gator, boarding
The boardwalk, shows our scornful pal
Its alimentary canal
And, with no help from electricity,
Demonstrates its authenticity.

Suzette Smart did something dumb:
Leaped upon the pendulum
Of the town hall's massive clock
For a swing ride. See her rock
To and fro, seasick and woozy—
Hourly, we hear from Suzie.

Though his friends with fearful squeals
Light out, taking to their heels,

Steadfast Abner doesn't blanch
At the rushing avalanche.

"What's a little pebble shower?
Go on, run, you yellow cowar——"

Stan said, "Guess I'll do some sewing—
Darn you, old machine, start going!"

Whiz!—it sewed him to his britches.
Now the doc has Stan in stitches.

At the dog show, Heloise
Empties sacks of frisky fleas
On Aunt Pru's prize Pekingese.

Poor little Peke, left hind leg pumping,
Starts to scratch, her point-score slumping,
But wins first place for hurdle-jumping

And then, as neatly as you please,
Shakes herself on Heloise.

Merely for a laugh, Lorraine
Yanked the cord that stopped the train,
Causing someone in the diner
To fall flat and get a shiner,
All the luggage in the racks
To smash down on people's backs.

Sweet Lorraine! She shrieked with laughter.
She's the one the cops came after.

Where the huge sea tortoise sits
On her sandpile tiptoes Fritz
(Who of all brats is the dregs),
Sack in hand to steal her eggs,
But, on tangling with Mom Tortoise,
Fritz comes down with rigor mortis.

Reggie, skilled at imitating
The *moos* of moose intent on mating,
Summons mobs of moose, all antlers,
Speedy Reginald-dismantlers.

In the kitchen Kitty Spender
Passes catfood through the blender

And to give it zing she tosses
In great shakes of spicy sauces.

"Yum!" says Dad, "this spread has spirit!
Why won't Tabby Cat come near it?"

Genevieve while Father tussles
With his barbell, building muscles,
Tosses a banana peel
Under his unwitting heel,
Causing him to skid and heave
A hundred pounds at Genevieve.

Yielding to his yen to roam,
Randolph ran away from home
For an eighteen-hour day
Fetching water, pitching hay
For a hungry elephant.
All day long he'd sweat and pant
And each night, though sorely tired,
From a cannon he'd be fired.
"Ow!" he groaned. "They sure do work us—
This here circus is no circus."

Stilts, the tallest ever built,
Still weren't tall enough for Milt,
So he nailed, with good intentions,
To both stilts ten-foot extensions.

Tall he towered, unafraid
Of dizzying height, but as he swayed
From side to side, from stilt to stilt,
Poor Milt's breakfast up and spilt.

On the golf course Gertrude spied
The kind of mower that you ride
Standing idle, jumped aboard,
Shifted gears and forward roared.

Round and round, that huge machinery
Circled, chewing up the greenery
Till a whole huge racetrack gaped,
All fresh mud and doughnut-shaped.

Gertrude said as she surveyed
Gleefully the mess she'd made,
"Gosh, but aren't golf courses fun?
See, I've made a hole in one!"

Quent, because Aunt Dru dreads quakes,
Gives her bed insistent shakes,
Rattles rocks in tin cans, bawling,
"Wake up, Aunt! The ceiling's falling!"—
But knowing well how Quent dissembles,
Aunt gives chase. The whole town trembles.

In his rotted rowboat, Rip
Rowed right to the roaring lip
Of a raging cataract,
Up against a boulder cracked,
Bounced shrill shrieks off canyon walls—

How pride goes before a falls!

On a factory tour, Will Gossage,
Watching folks make bratwurst sausage,
Jumped into the meat feet-first.

Brats are bad, but Will's the wurst.

Harkness parked his howling hound
In his homeroom's lost-and-found.

When poor Teacher tried to teach,
It let out a piercing screech

And a loud *Ow-oo! Ow-oo!*—
No one knew what's two times two.

Teacher, since it kept on baying,
Cried, "I quit! Go home, start playing!"